The best of
JAMES RAE

Exploring popular musical styles for alto saxophone

UE 21 408
ISMN 979-0-008-07917-7
UPC 8-03452-06277-6
ISBN 978-3-7024-6559-9

© Copyright 2008 by Universal Edition A.G., Wien

Contents – Inhalt – Table des Matières

Ragtime 7
The Roll-Over Rag 9
A Pocket-Size Rag 10

Swing and the Walking Bass 13
Deal Me In! 15
Passin' Through 16
Full On 17

The Blues 19
Yesterday's Blues 21
Back Shift 22

Latin 23
Tradewinds 25
Matt's New Motor 26
Blue Cockatoo 28

Jazz Waltz 29
Waltz for Emily 31
Situation Comedy 32
Groove It! 34

Ballad 35
Low Tide 37
Song Without Words 38

Rock 41
The Guv'nor 43
Bruno's Tune 44
Sax Un-Plugged 45

Folk 47
His Father's Son 49
A Drop O' the Hard Stuff 50

Charleston & Showtime 51
Bottoms Up! 53
Curtain Up! 54

Preface

As a professional freelance woodwind player, I have had the good fortune to have been involved in practical music making in many different settings ranging from contemporary classical concerts to West End musicals. This collection of pieces, for elementary to intermediate level players, is selected from the many I have composed over the years for my pupils, inspired by my own first-hand experience as a performer.

Most of these pieces, drawn from a variety of publications on style and technical skills, are appearing here for the first time with CD. Players are offered a range of entertaining and challenging material for using over a considerable period of time and all, with the exception of the studies, with stylish and supportive accompaniments for using at home. For listening purposes, and to encourage a good feeling for style, each accompaniment track is preceded by a demonstration performance of the piece. I have also recorded performances of the studies.

Teachers too will find this collection a useful resource. The piano accompaniments are 'teacher friendly' and include chord symbols for those who wish to simplify or elaborate.

Use this book to explore various styles, play-along with the CD – and enjoy it!

James Rae
October 2007

Vorwort

Als professioneller Holzbläser hatte ich das Glück, an vielen unterschiedlichen Musikproduktionen beteiligt gewesen zu sein, von zeitgenössischen klassischen Konzerten bis hin zu Londoner West End-Musicals. Die vorliegende Ausgabe von Spielstücken für Anfänger und leicht Fortgeschrittene enthält eine Auswahl, die ich über Jahre hinweg für meine Schüler komponiert habe, inspiriert von meinen eigenen Erfahrungen als Künstler.

Die meisten dieser Stücke, zusammengestellt aus einer Reihe von Heften über musikalische Stile und instrumentale Spieltechniken, wurden hier erstmalig auf CD eingespielt. Musikerinnen und Musikern wird eine große Bandbreite von unterhaltsamem und anspruchsvollem Material geboten, das über eine lange Zeitspanne hinweg im Unterricht oder im Selbststudium verwendet werden kann. Für alle Stücke mit Ausnahme der Etüden für Solosaxophon gibt es stilgerechte und unterstützende Begleitmusik für das Spielen zu Hause. Zum Anhören und um ein Gefühl für Stil zu entwickeln, ist jedem Play-Along-Track eine Vollversion des Stückes vorangestellt. Die Stücke für Solosaxophon habe ich als Referenz ebenfalls aufgenommen.

Auch Lehrer werden diese Ausgabe gut verwenden können. Die Klavierbegleitungen sind leicht zu spielen und mit Akkordsymbolen für diejenigen, die sie vereinfachen oder weiter ausarbeiten möchten, versehen.

Viel Spaß mit diesem Buch wünscht

James Rae
Oktober 2007

Préface

En tant qu'interprète professionnel et indépendant d'instruments à vent en bois, j'ai eu la chance de participer à toutes sortes de mises en scène, de concerts classiques contemporains jusqu'à des comédies musicales West-End. Ce recueil de pièces de niveau débutant/débutant avancé est une sélection parmi les nombreux morceaux que j'ai composés pour mes élèves au fil des ans, sur la base de mon expérience d'interprète.

La plupart de ces pièces, extraites d'une variété de publications sur le style et les connaissances techniques, font ici pour la première fois l'objet d'un CD. Les interprètes disposent ainsi d'un matériel divertissant et stimulant dont ils pourront profiter pendant longtemps. Des accompagnements à la fois plaisants et efficaces sont proposés avec l'ensemble du matériel musical, à l'exception des études. Chaque morceau de musique d'accompagnement est d'abord joué pour exercer l'oreille et développer la sensibilité au style. Pour la même raison, j'ai également enregistré les études.

Les enseignants apprécieront eux aussi le côté utile de cette collection. Les accompagnements au piano sont «faciles à utiliser» et contiennent la désignation des accords pour ceux qui souhaitent simplifier, voire élaborer.

Ce livre est une invitation à explorer de nombreux styles, jouez tout en écoutant le CD – et passez des moments agréables!

James Rae
Octobre 2007

Ragtime

Ragtime, contrary to popular belief, has very little to do with jazz. In fact Scott Joplin, arguably the greatest exponent of compositions in this style, did not like his music to be classified as jazz. The main interpretive difference being that ragtime generally utilises straight (even) quaver and semi-quaver movement, as in classical and even rock music, as opposed to the swing style commonly used in jazz. Stylistically, much of the rhythmic energy in ragtime comes from the use of heavily syncopated melodies over a regular 'um-cha, um-cha' accompaniment. Always aim to observe all accents and articulation marks when playing such pieces in order to capture the true character of the music.

Ragtime

Im Gegensatz zur weit verbreiteten Ansicht hat Ragtime wenig mit Jazz zu tun. Scott Joplin, der wohl bedeutendste Vertreter dieses Stils, mochte es beispielsweise nicht, wenn seine Musik als Jazz bezeichnet wurde. Bei der Interpretation liegt der Hauptunterschied darin, dass Ragtime im Allgemeinen gerade (gleichmäßige) Achtel- und Sechzehntelbewegungen verwendet, wie in der klassischen Musik und sogar im Rock, im Gegensatz zum üblicherweise mit einer Swing-Phrasierung gespielten Jazz. Stilistisch gesehen geht ein großer Teil der rhythmischen Energie des Ragtime aus der Verwendung stark synkopierter Melodien über einer regelmäßigen „um-tscha, um-tscha"-Begleitung hervor. Versuchen Sie beim Spielen solcher Stücke immer, alle Akzente und Phrasierungsmarkierungen zu beachten, um das Wesen der Musik zu erfassen.

Le ragtime

Malgré une opinion largement répandue, le ragtime a bien peu de points communs avec le jazz. Scott Joplin, par exemple, qui est certainement le plus grand compositeur de ce style, n'aimait pas voir sa musique qualifiée de jazz. La principale différence réside dans l'interprétation : alors que le ragtime se sert en général de mouvements de croches et de doubles croches directes (parallèles), à l'instar de la musique classique et même du rock, le jazz est habituellement joué dans le style swing. Stylistiquement, une grande partie de l'énergie rythmique du ragtime provient de l'utilisation de mélodies lourdement syncopées sur un accompagnement «um-cha, um-cha» régulier. Essayez toujours de respecter tous les accents et marques d'articulation en jouant ce type de morceaux afin de capter le caractère véritable de la musique.

for saxophone and piano:

Track 2/3 *The Roll-Over Rag* from *Introducing the Saxophone Plus – Book 2* [UE 30421]

Track 4/5 *A Pocket-Size Rag* from *Jazzy Saxophone 2* [UE 19362]

The Roll-Over Rag

James Rae

© Copyright 1997 by Universal Edition (London) Ltd., London

UE 21408

A Pocket-Size Rag

James Rae

© Copyright 1990 by Universal Edition (London) Ltd., London

UE 21408

Swing and the Walking Bass

Swing is the most common style used in jazz music. Nowadays it is mostly written as standard quavers with a text or notational indication saying that they should be swung, e.g 'Easy swing feel' etc. This means that the first of every two quavers on the beat is lengthened and the second shortened at a ratio of 2 to 1. i.e. Two thirds of a crotchet followed by one third respectively. This also applies very importantly to the rests as many phrases in jazz start after a rest. As well as changing the rhythm, it is also stylistically correct to stress the shorter of the two quavers in order to give the music a feeling of 'swagger'.

Swing und Walking-Bass

Swing ist der am weitesten verbreitete Stil im Jazz. Heutzutage werden meist „normale" Achtelnoten notiert, wobei ein Anmerkung darauf hinweist, dass sie „swingend" gespielt werden sollen, z.B. „Leichtes Swing-Feel". Dies bedeutet, dass jeweils die erste von zwei Achtelnoten einer Schlageinheit verlängert und die zweite im Verhältnis von 2 zu 1 verkürzt wird, d.h. zwei Drittel einer Viertelnote, gefolgt von jeweils einem Drittel. Es ist sehr wichtig, dies auch für die Pausen anzuwenden, da viele Phrasen im Jazz nach einem Pausenzeichen beginnen. Ebenso wie eine Änderung des Rhythmus ist es auch stilistisch korrekt, die kürzere der beiden Achtelnoten zu betonen, um der Musik ein gewisses „Wiegen" zu verleihen.

Swing et walking bass

Le swing est le style le plus fréquemment utilisé par le jazz. Aujourd'hui, il est le plus souvent écrit en croches standard, avec une remarque ou une note indiquant qu'elles doivent être jouées avec swing, p.ex. «Easy swing feel» etc. Ceci signifie que la première de chaque paire de croches d'une mesure est rallongée et la deuxième raccourcie dans un rapport de 2 à 1. Autrement dit, deux tiers de croche sont à chaque fois suivis d'un tiers. Il est primordial d'appliquer ceci également aux pauses, puisque dans le jazz, nombre de mouvements commencent après une pause. Tout comme un changement de rythme, le style permet également d'accentuer la plus courte des deux croches pour conférer à la musique un mouvement de balancement.

for saxophone and piano:

💿 Track 6/7   *Deal Me In!* from *Easy Jazzy Saxophone* [UE 16 578]

💿 Track 8/9   *Passin' Through* from *Easy Jazzy Saxophone* [UE 16 578]

for saxophone solo:

💿 Track 10   *Full On* from *Style Workout* [UE 21 232]

Deal Me In!

James Rae

© Copyright 1995 by Universal Edition (London) Ltd., London

UE 21408

Passin' Through

James Rae

Full On

James Rae

The Blues

Blues music can be found in a wide variety of styles including both swing and rock. Most blues melodies tend to fall into the standard twelve-bar structure and often include notes of the blues scale. The flattened third, seventh and, strongest of all, fifth give the music its distinctive character. When playing blues pieces, always be aware of the underlying accompaniment, and at the same time aim to be flexible and very expressive within the regular pulse. Don't be afraid to bend the odd note here and there but try not to over-do it!

Der Blues

Blues kann in vielen verschiedenen Stilen gefunden werden, einschließlich Swing und Rock. Die meisten Blues-Melodien fallen in die übliche zwölftaktige Form und enthalten meist Töne der Bluestonleiter. Die erniedrigte Terz, Septime und vor allem die Quinte als stärkstes Intervall geben der Musik ihren markanten Charakter. Seien Sie sich beim Spielen von Blues-Stücken immer der begleitenden Akkorde bewusst, und versuchen Sie gleichzeitig innerhalb des regelmäßigen Pulses flexibel und sehr ausdrucksstark zu sein. Zögern Sie nicht, hie und da die eine oder andere Note zu „verziehen", aber versuchen Sie, es nicht zu übertreiben!

Le blues

Le blues présente une grande variété de styles, y compris le swing et le rock. La plupart des mélodies de blues ont tendance à s'inscrire dans la structure standard des douze mesures et incluent souvent des notes de la gamme de blues. La tierce baissée, la septième et la quinte en tant qu'intervalle le plus marqué procurent à la musique son caractère puissant. En jouant des morceaux de blues, soyez toujours conscient de l'accompagnement sous-jacent, et essayez en même temps de rester souple et particulièrement expressif au sein de l'impulsion régulière. N'hésitez pas à tordre une note par ci et par là, sans toutefois trop exagérer !

for saxophone and piano:

Track 11/12 *Yesterday's Blues* from *Introducing the Saxophone Plus – Book 1* [UE 30420]

Track 13/14 *Back Shift* from *Easy Blue Saxophone* [UE 21262]

Yesterday's Blues

James Rae

© Copyright 1997 by Universal Edition (London) Ltd., London

UE 21408

Back Shift

James Rae

Latin

Latin American music, like the blues, comes in many styles ranging from cool bossa-novas to hot driving sambas. It is rhythmically the most highly-charged music on the planet! Unlike blues however, it does not include swing. Latin music has to be played with a great deal of energy as it is essentially dance music. Try to capture this style in your playing by carefully observing and exaggerating all of the articulation markings in order to make it sound larger than life.

Latin

Genau wie der Blues besteht die lateinamerikanische Musik aus vielen Stilen, von den kühlen Bossa Novas bis hin zu den heißen Sambas! Rhythmisch gesehen ist es die temperamentvollste Musik der Welt! Im Gegensatz zum Blues gibt es im Latin keine Swing-Phrasierung. Latin-Musik muss mit sehr viel Energie gespielt werden, da es sich vor allem um Tanzmusik handelt. Versuchen Sie, den Stil in seiner Spielweise zu erfassen, indem Sie alle Phrasierungsanweisungen genau beachten und manchmal sogar übertreiben, damit die Musik lebendig klingt.

Latin

La musique de l'Amérique latine affiche, tout comme le blues, une variété de styles allant des froides bossa-novas aux brûlantes sambas. Au niveau du rythme, nous voilà confrontés à la musique la plus explosive de la planète ! Toutefois, contrairement au blues, le swing n'en fait pas partie. Comme il s'agit essentiellement de musique de dance, la musique latine est à jouer avec dynamisme. Essayez de capter ce style dans votre jeu en respectant et en exagérant toutes les marques d'articulation pour que la musique sonne plus grand que nature.

for saxophone and piano:

🎵 Track 15/16 *Tradewinds* from *Latin Saxophone* [UE 17 364]

🎵 Track 17/18 *Matt's New Motor* from *Take Another Ten – Saxophone* [UE 21 170]

for solo saxophone:

🎵 Track 19 *Blue Cockatoo* from *Style Workout* [UE 21 232]

Tradewinds

James Rae

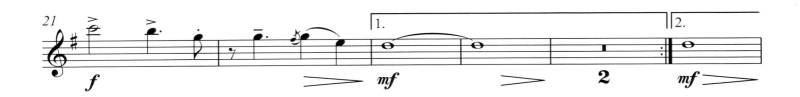
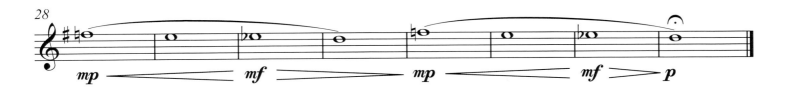

© Copyright 1998 by Universal Edition (London) Ltd., London

Matt's New Motor

James Rae

© Copyright 2003 by Universal Edition (London) Ltd., London

UE 21408

Blue Cockatoo

James Rae

Jazz Waltz

Cool is the name of the game here! Jazz waltzes are usually written in a fast swing triple time. Always try to feel where the downbeat falls as it comes one beat earlier than pieces written in 4/4 time. In practice, this means that the bars will appear to fly past very quickly so always read well ahead and anticipate what is coming up. Oh, and by the way, don't forget to keep the quavers swinging throughout! (see Swing section)

Der Jazz Waltz

Cool sein ist hier angesagt! Jazz-Walzer sind normalerweise in einem schnellen Swing-Dreiertakt geschrieben. Versuchen Sie die schwere Zählzeit zu erspüren, denn sie kommt einen Schlag früher als bei den Stücken im Vierviertaltakt. Praktisch gesehen bedeutet dies, dass die Takte sehr schnell vorbeizufliegen scheinen, lesen Sie also immer weit voraus und bereiten Sie sich auf die folgenden Töne vor. Und vergessen Sie außerdem nicht, die Achtelnoten das ganze Stück über swingen zu lassen! (siehe Kapitel Swing)

Le Jazz Waltz

Le détachement, voilà l'essentiel ici! Les valses de jazz sont généralement écrites dans une mesure swing rapide à trois temps. Essayez toujours de sentir où tombe le geste conclusif qui vient une mesure plus tôt que dans les morceaux en mesure à quatre-quatre. En pratique, ceci signifie que les mesures auront l'air de passer très rapidement. Lisez donc toujours bien en avance et anticipez. Et n'oubliez surtout pas de swinger les croches! (voir rubrique Swing)

for saxophone and piano:

⊙ Track 20/21   *Waltz for Emily* from *Blue Saxophone* [UE 19 765]

⊙ Track 22/23   *Situation Comedy* from *Take Ten – Saxophone* [UE 18 836]

for solo saxophone:

⊙ Track 24   *Groove it!* from *20 Modern Studies* [UE 18 820]

Waltz for Emily

James Rae

Situation Comedy

James Rae

© Copyright 1989 by Universal Edition (London) Ltd., London

Groove It!

James Rae

Ballad

Ballads are generally slower, lyrical pieces that need a great deal of thought when it comes to interpretation. They have to be played in a very expressive manner as if you are telling a story through the music. This is so important as they can often sound dull and half-hearted if the player simply 'goes through the motions' and merely plays the notes on the page. As in the blues pieces, don't be afraid to bend the occasional note and also experiment with using many different colours in your sound production in order to capture the interest of your audience.

Die Ballade

Balladen sind im Allgemeinen langsame, lyrische Stücke, deren Aufführung gründlicher Vorbereitung bedürfen. Sie müssen sehr ausdrucksvoll gespielt werden, als würde der Spieler durch die Musik eine Geschichte erzählen. Dies ist sehr wichtig, weil die Stücke oft langweilig und halbherzig klingen können, wenn der Spieler die Töne „herunterrasselt" und nur die Noten spielt, die geschrieben stehen. Zögern Sie nicht, genau wie bei den Blues-Stücken hie und da einen Ton zu verbiegen und zu experimentieren, indem Sie beim Erzeugen der Töne viele verschiedene Klangfarben einsetzen, um das Interesse des Publikums zu wecken.

Ballad

Les ballades sont en général des pièces plus lentes, plus lyriques dont l'interprétation exige une grande réflexion. Elles doivent être jouées avec expression comme si vous racontiez une histoire à travers la musique. Ceci est particulièrement important, étant donné qu'elles peuvent être ennuyeuses et vides d'enthousiasme si l'interprète «parcourt» seulement les mouvements et ne joue que les notes qui se trouvent sur la page. N'hésitez pas, tout comme dans les morceaux de blues, de tordre une note de temps à autre et d'expérimenter en produisant des sons enrichis de votre touche personnelle afin d'éveiller l'intérêt du public.

for saxophone and piano:

Track 25/26 *Low Tide* from *Easy Jazzy Saxophone* [UE 16 578]

Track 27/28 *Song Without Words* from *Jazzy Saxophone 2* [UE 19 362]

Low Tide

James Rae

Song Without Words

James Rae

© Copyright 1990 by Universal Edition (London) Ltd., London

Rock

Now you get a chance to really let your hair down! Rock music is often aggressive and has to be played in a very powerful manner. Don't hold back, just let rip! The saxophone can do everything an electric guitar can in this style of music – only better! Warning! You have in your hands a musical weapon capable of turning heads at a hundred yards! Keep it big, keep it mean but always keep it under control. Listen to your intonation as it is easy to get carried away by sheer volume and lose your sense of pitch. (Horrible!)

Rock

Jetzt bekommen Sie die Gelegenheit, sich richtig auszutoben! Rock-Musik ist oft aggressiv und muss kraftvoll gespielt werden. Seien Sie nicht zurückhaltend, legen Sie einfach los! Das Saxophon kann bei dieser Musik alles vollbringen, wozu auch eine E-Gitarre in der Lage ist – nur noch besser! Achtung! Sie haben eine musikalische Waffe in Ihren Händen, mit der Sie in einem Umkreis von fast 100 Metern Leuten den Kopf verdrehen können! Lassen Sie es ordentlich krachen, heizen Sie Ihrem Publikum ein, aber behalten Sie die Kontrolle. Konzentrieren Sie sich auf Ihre Tongebung, da man schnell durch die Lautstärke allein mitgerissen wird und das Gefühl für Tonhöhe und Intonation verliert. (Fürchterlich!)

Rock

A présent, voici l'occasion de vous relâcher complètement! La musique rock est souvent agressive et doit être jouée avec force. Ne vous retenez pas, déchaînez-vous! Dans ce style de musique, le saxophone peut produire tous les sons d'une guitare électrique – encore mieux! Mais attention, vous avez en main une véritable arme musicale capable de tourner les têtes dans un périmètre d'environ 100 mètres! Faites un bruit d'enfer, mettez de l'ambiance mais ne perdez jamais le contrôle. Ecoutez votre intonation, car le volume seul risque de vous emporter et de vous faire perdre le sens de la hauteur du son. (Horrible!)

for saxophone and piano:

Track 29/30   *The Guv'nor* from *Play it Cool – Saxophone* [UE 21 404]

Track 31/32   *Bruno's Tune* from *Play it Cool – Saxophone* [UE 21 404]

for solo saxophone:

Track 33   *Sax Un-plugged* from *Style Workout* [UE 21 232]

The Guv'nor

James Rae

Bruno's Tune

James Rae

© Copyright 2002 by Universal Edition (London) Ltd., London

UE 21408

Sax Un-Plugged

James Rae

Folk

The saxophone, on the face of it, is not an instrument that instantly springs to mind when talking about folk music. However, because of its great expressiveness and agility it is very much at home in this genre. An excellent example of this was the use of the soprano saxophone in the blockbuster show 'Riverdance'. In many ways folk music is like classical music in terms of interpretation and has to be played in a very controlled yet expressive style with great technical accuracy.

Folk

Wenn von Folk-Musik die Rede ist, denkt man nicht sofort an das Saxophon. Dennoch hat es aufgrund seiner Ausdrucksstärke und seiner Lebendigkeit in diesem Genre seinen Platz. Ein hervorragendes Beispiel hierfür ist der Gebrauch des Sopransaxophons in der Blockbuster-Show „Riverdance". In Bezug auf die Interpretation ist Folk-Musik in vieler Hinsicht wie klassische Musik zu sehen, und muss in einem kontrollierten, aber gleichzeitig ausdrucksstarken Stil mit großer technischer Genauigkeit gespielt werden.

Folk

A première vue, le saxophone n'est pas l'instrument qui vient immédiatement à l'esprit lorsqu'on évoque la musique folk. Néanmoins, grâce à sa force d'expression et à sa vivacité, il y est bien à sa place. L'utilisation du saxophone soprano dans le fameux show «Riverdance» en est un excellent exemple. A de nombreux égards, la musique folk ressemble à la musique classique sur le plan de l'interprétation. Elle doit être contrôlée tout en permettant un jeu expressif et une grande précision technique.

for saxophone and piano:

Track 34/35 *His Father's Son* from *Sounds Irish* [UE 21 080]

Track 36/37 *A Drop O' the Hard Stuff* from *Sounds Irish* [UE 21 080]

His Father's Son

James Rae

A Drop O' the Hard Stuff

James Rae

Charleston & Showtime

The saxophone really comes to the fore in dance-orientated pieces. Charleston and showtime are both energetic two-in-a-bar styles from the early twentieth century when saxophones could be found in great abundance in dance and music hall bands. This music is the next development after ragtime and before swing where things moved into a four-in-a-bar feel. Always aim to keep this music moving along as the bars pass very rapidly only having two beats each. Try to highlight all of the accents in order to really punctuate the syncopated rhythms.

Charleston & Showtime

Das Saxophon rückt bei tanzorientierten Stücken richtig in den Vordergrund. Charleston und Showtime sind energiegeladene zwei-taktige Stile des frühen zwanzigsten Jahrhunderts, als Saxophone noch in großer Anzahl in Tanz- und Musikensembles zu finden waren. Diese Musik entwickelte sich nach dem Ragtime und vor dem Swing, mit dem der Vierteltakt etabliert wurde. Bemühen Sie sich stets, diese Musik voran zu treiben, da die Takte mit nur zwei Schlägen schnell vorbei sind. Versuchen Sie, alle Akzente zu betonen, um die synkopierten Rhythmen zu unterstreichen.

Charleston & Showtime

Le saxophone s'impose réellement dans les pièces axées sur la danse. Charleston et Showtime sont tous deux des styles dynamiques sur une mesure à deux temps, nés au début du vingtième siècle, alors que les saxophones abondaient dans les groupes de dance et de concert. Cette musique s'est développée après le ragtime et avant le swing, qui a tout fait passer à la mesure à quatre temps. Veillez à toujours garder cette musique en mouvement. Les mesures passent très rapidement, étant donné que chacune n'a que deux temps. Essayez de souligner tous les accents afin de bien accentuer les rythmes syncopés.

for saxophone and piano:

⊙ Track 38/39 *Bottoms Up!* from *Introducing the Saxophone Plus – Book 2* [UE 30421]

⊙ Track 40/41 *Curtain Up!* from *Play it Cool – Saxophone* [UE 21404]

Bottoms Up!

James Rae

© Copyright 1997 by Universal Edition (London) Ltd., London

UE 21408

Curtain Up!

James Rae

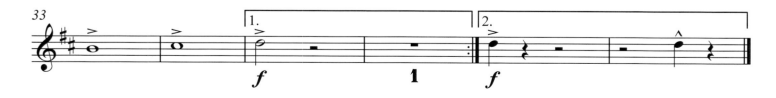

© Copyright 2002 by Universal Edition (London) Ltd., London

UE 21408

A selection of saxophone titles by James Rae

Easy

Introducing the Saxophone Plus Book 1 (alto sax & pno)	UE 30 420
Eyes & Ears Saxophone Level 1 – Sight-reading (2 sax)	UE 21 144
Easy Blue Saxophone (alto or tenor sax & pno)	UE 21 262
Easy Jazzy Saxophone (alto or tenor sax & pno)	UE 16 578
Easy Jazzy Duets (2 sax)	UE 16 551
Play it Cool – Saxophone (alto or tenor sax & pno or CD)	UE 21 100
Easy Studies in Jazz and Rock (sax)	UE 19 392

Easy to Intermediate

Introducing the Saxophone (Engl.) (alto sax + CD)	UE 17 390
James Rae's Methode für Saxophon (Dt.) (Altsax.+ CD)	UE 31 499
Introducing the Saxophone Plus Book 2 (alto sax & pno)	UE 30 421
Introducing Saxophone – Duets (2 sax)	UE 21 359
Introducing Saxophone – Trios (3 sax)	UE 21 360
Introducing Saxophone – Quartets (4 sax)	UE 21 361
Eyes & Ears Saxophone Level 2 – Sight-reading (2 sax)	UE 21 145
Style Workout – Saxophone (sax)	UE 21 232
20 Modern Studies (sax)	UE 18 820
Jazz Scale Studies (sax)	UE 21 353
Latin Saxophone (alto or tenor sax & pno)	UE 17 364
Jazz Zone (alto or tenor sax + CD)	UE 21 030
Sounds Irish (alto or tenor sax & pno)	UE 21 080

Intermediate

Blue Saxophone (alto or tenor sax & pno)	UE 19 765
Jazzy Saxophone 1 (alto or tenor sax & pno)	UE 18 827
Jazzy Saxophone 2 (alto or tenor sax & pno)	UE 19 362
Jazzy Duets (2 sax)	UE 19 395
Take Ten (alto sax & pno)	UE 18 836
Take Another Ten (sax & pno)	UE 21 170

EYES & EARS
by James Rae

For Developing Sight-Reading Skills through Duet-Playing

This unique series in four volumes from Foundation to Advanced, presents carefully graded material with TOP TIPS and advice from James Rae along the way. With the development of keen eyes and ears and using the 'five golden rules' explained in each book, the player is equipped with a strategy with which to approach an unfamiliar piece of music. With the resulting increase in confidence and the support from the teacher's duet part, sight-reading can become an enjoyable challenge. Concluding each book, specimen tests are set as encountered in a typical examination.

Eyes & Ears – Saxophone

UE 21 144	**Foundation**	Grades 1–2
UE 21 145	**The next step**	Grades 3–4
UE 21 146	**Intermediate**	Grades 5–6
UE 21 196	**Advanced**	Grades 7–8

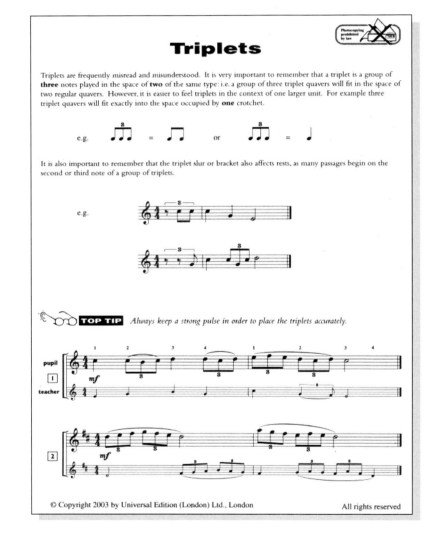

'We can be eternally grateful for people like James Rae ... for providing us with so much educational material that is well thought through and progressive ... splendid books ... and can be recommended without hesitation ... this is an invaluable set.'

Gordon Egerton, reviewing Eyes & Ears – Clarinet for MUSIC TEACHER

vienna • london • new york